World Building for Fiction Writers

Vicky Burkholder

CONTENTS

INTRODUCTION

I have been a writer and editor for twenty years and a reader for much longer than that. As such, I have seen books that succeed or fail based on the world building done by the author. Whether you write science fiction, fantasy, contemporary romances, or historical works, all of them require you to build a setting that the reader can believe in. Do you want a Muggle world up against a magic world? Then make me believe it can actually exist. Is your story set in the Americas in the 1700s? Put me there. Set on a lifeless moon? Give me a space suit or a habitat that I can accept as fact. Set in today's world? Your reader may not know the quirks and sayings that are common in your area. For that matter, you might not either unless you do your research. Getting it right is world building.

To illustrate, I just finished editing a story set in California near the middle of the state. The characters were all native Californians and there was nothing non-California about the story. But... the author was obviously British because the terminology he used was all Brit-speak. Lifts for elevators, car park for parking lot, torch for flashlight, trainers for sneakers. It was a good story, but it completely failed because the terminology was all wrong. The author didn't world-build.

One of the exciting challenges of writing is building your world. It doesn't matter if you write science fiction, fantasy, historical fiction or contemporary fiction—you need to build your world. If you do happen to write fantasy or science fiction, it's even more important. You are not only in control of the dialogue and background of your characters, but of every aspect of their lives. If they get bitten by an insect, it's there because you created it. If they must live on an ice-covered planet, you control the weather.

Actually, you control every aspect of your characters' lives, no matter where or when they are so you need to know the world they're in.

For those who write contemporary or historical fiction, you must create your worlds within the bounds of what really exists in our world and when it existed. Unless you want irate readers writing nasty letters about inaccuracies, you have to use what there is and not imagine new things. There are strict limitations on what your characters wear, how they travel, the laws and social customs where they live. You can control their dress, actions, speech, etc., but you must remain true to what is real and exists in our world.

There are fewer restrictions when writing speculative fiction. Humans are still humans and, as such, should breathe air (unless they've been genetically altered, in which case, they aren't strictly human), but all other aspects of their lives are yours to control.

"That's easy," you say. "I'll just put them in this world, add a few phasers and hovercars and I'll have a futuristic." Or add wizards and a quest and a fantasy will emerge. Make them psychically active or add ghosts and you have a paranormal.

Yes, you can do this. But... the richness of detail will be missing unless you've done your homework. Take a look at J.K. Rowling's "Harry Potter" books. The societies she builds are rich in detail. The Muggle, or real world, and the wizard world have separate currencies, methods of travel, mores, laws, and even mail delivery. The richness of the two worlds lies in the details she gives us. Without them, the books wouldn't be nearly as good as they are.

"The devil is in the details" is an often used quote in writing classes and seminars. And it's very true. Details ground your reader in your world, no matter where or when it is. The following parts will help you develop your worlds. You'll have a ton of material, most of which you won't use. So why do all the work? To ground yourself in your world. The more you know about your world, the easier it will be to write. You'll use it subconsciously and it will show in the flow of your writing. You may have a character who climbs a hill. Does she see a village below? Or a hamlet on an island in the middle of a raging river that is accessible only by a magic spell? Your writing will reflect the work you have done, even if you're not aware of it.

You can spend an inordinate amount of time creating your world, but if I can't smell the tangy scent of a flower, then you haven't created a real place. The reader has to believe this world to be real—even if it's not. In addition to the world, cities, towns, etc., there should be areas like bars or taverns, spaceports, gardens, parks, etc. where the reader really feels "at home,". World building isn't just about creating a cool new world but about making the reader feel like s/he could live there. That they could be transported to that world and feel that it is real.

It will also pay off as you write the story by helping you remember who wears what type of clothing, how they speak, what they look like, etc. Halfway into your story, you don't want to have to stop and dig back through previous chapters to find out that the Ramsers used florikins for money and not sporates as the Shankars do.

But what about historical or contemporary stories? Why do you need this information? You need it to make certain your world is historically accurate or that you don't introduce anomalies to your story. If you live in central Iowa but write about Scottish clans and highland flings, you need to know what kind of money they use, how they dress, what the lay of the lands is, and all the information to make your book accurate.

Are you going to set your story in the here and now? In the area where you live? Check out the idiomatic speech of your area. Speech patterns vary widely from one area to the next. Does your heroine eat a hoagie, grinder, sub, hero, or Blimpie? Does she drink soda, cola, coke, or pop? Does she use a gum band or a rubber band? These are all things that you need to know in order to write accurate details. And trust me, readers will notice if you're wrong.

Even when you do create your world, you have to know what's the same and what's different in your world. If you write about technology, be sure you know what's already going on in our world so you can ramp it up a little. If you write historical, know the history of the era you're in – even if it's an alternate universe. If you write about planets and novae, know what's already out there in our universe—and make sure you get the placement right.

If there are differences between our world and yours, be sure you let the reader in on them. Readers will believe what you tell them about your world, but only if you give them a reason to believe it.

And be sure you keep it consistent. If you create something...keep it the same throughout the story unless you give us a very good reason why not. Make your world part of your story. If you are going to all the trouble of creating one, let the reader see it through the story.

Remember when you put people in your world to keep them real. People are the result of their environment, past, history, and a lot more. If you create aliens, be sure they're not just crazy humans in stupid costumes. Make them products of their environments, history, and more. Make your reader want to go there to visit (or not, depending on the environment). Make the people nice for the most part (yes, you can have villains—that's a given), but not everyone is a villain. Give them fun things to look at, to do, to eat and drink. Harry Potter had Quidditch, Butterbeer, and more. Have fun with it.

Technology and societies don't change overnight, but through years. Yes, sometimes it seems like things happen fast—and sometimes they do—but for the most part, it takes a long time for things to change.

One caveat I will leave you with—don't feel that you have to completely fill the questions in each section completely. Sometimes, less is more. You need to build your world but you don't have to give us every single detail. You're not writing an encyclopedia here—unless you want to for a reason. Give your reader enough to ground them in your world, but don't overwhelm them with details. There should be enough to put us there, but we don't need to know everything. Find the balance between details and overwhelming.

It's time to roll up your sleeves and prepare to do some work, and have fun with it. As you go through the sections, you will find many places that overlap. That's the way of life. The weather affects what plants grow and animals live, which affects the people, which affects the transportation, etc. Work through the sections and, at the end, you will have a place, people, and culture that is uniquely yours. The book is laid out as a series of questions. Answer the questions and you'll have your world.

Let's build a world.

CHAPTER 1: THE PHYSICAL WORLD

GEOGRAPHY

In working through this section, I am going to assume you've got the science right and that the world you're creating can exist within our physical universe. If not, there are several excellent (though technical) books and websites that can guide you through what you need to know—from types of stars necessary to sustain life as we know it, optimal orbital distance, atmospheric makeup, satellites, etc. We're going to start a few steps beyond those details. I'll give general guidelines in the pages and at the end are questions you can go through for in depth creation.

General:

Where exactly will your story take place? Most fantasy stories occur on Earth-like worlds. The laws of physics may not apply if wizards and fantasy creatures roam the land, but the world is basically similar to ours. Science fiction allows a bit more leeway since your characters may live on a space station, a lifeless moon, or even an asteroid. Wherever you put your characters, they are still going to have to know what their surroundings look like. As the writer, you need to know how much ground your story is going to cover. Will your characters stay in one place (not usually a good idea unless you're writing a short story), or move around? The first thing you need to determine is how much space you will cover in your story. Will it be in a single city or encompass a continent or even multiple worlds? Once you decide how much space you'll need, you can play with what it looks like.

The Lay of the Land (Topography)

It's time to get out your drawing pad, erector set, Lego Building Blocks, modeling clay, or whatever you want to use to create your world in concrete form. For my first novel, I sat at the beach with my children and created my country in the sand. Sitting in the sun, we worked out problems with travel, why the land lay as it did, where the rivers, land, towns and more were and all sorts of other issues. A few snaps of my camera allowed me to take it home with me where I recreated it on paper. Others use salt dough or modeling clay (or mashed potatoes as in the movie Close Encounters of the Third Kind). Whatever medium works best for you, get it out and have some fun. This is your world.

Why do this? While it's not necessary, sometimes it does help to have a concrete image in front of you when you're working. If nothing else, you can move your characters around on the model as you move them through your story. You need for them to cross a river but they're too far north? You can either move them or the river and the diorama can help you with this. It's more than a visual aid, it's also a way to actually work the land and the story. It gives you a 3-D representation of your world.

What do you do if you're not into models? Draw a map. It doesn't have to be perfect. If you're artistically challenged, as I am, use an existing map of anywhere in the world and trace the outline onto new paper. Add your own features and names. It doesn't have to be perfect. This is a visual aid for you, no one else.

Once you've got the basic outline of your land, you need to add features. What does the land look like? How will the topography affect travel, communication, and so on? Distance between populations affects the way people get news to each other, how they get around, and the length of time it takes to do these things.

Climate affects landscape through erosion and weathering as well as the distribution of plants and animals, thus affecting what plants grow where, what animals live where, and what clothes people wear? And what about winds and oceans? These two work together to affect climate. They interact to affect weather—as in storms, droughts, or pleasant conditions.

One important thing to remember is that planets are rarely made of one thing. We don't have planets that are all ice or deserts or tropical. There should be variety on your planet. Even variety within countries.

QUESTIONS:

1. Where will the story take place?
2. How much ground will it cover?
3. If an alternate universe, how do extra moons or other differences affect the climate?
4. Are the laws of nature and physics the same there as in our world? If not, what are they like?
5. How do differences affect the planet? E.g. Multiple moons, suns, high tides, extra seasons, etc.
6. If there are non-human sentient people, what areas do they claim?
7. Where are the most/least populated areas? Why?
8. What does the land look like?
9. Are there hills, mountains, lakes, rivers, oceans or other features? Steep or low-lying?
10. Where are the most striking features and what are they? (Like the Grand Canyon in the US, Ayers Rock in Australia, Mt. Fuji in Japan, the Amazon or Nile River)
11. Are there volcanoes? Live or dormant? How often do they erupt?
12. How will the lay of the land affect travel and communication?
13. How much land is in each of the zones (polar, temperate, equatorial)?
14. Which areas are the most fertile farmland?
15. Where are the mineral resources located? Which ones are the most abundant? Which ones are scarce?
16. Are there places where there are rich deposits that haven't yet been discovered? Are there areas where they've been depleted?
17. Which ones are the most valuable? Why?
18. What water resources are available and are they used for anything?
19. How are the continents laid out? What is the ratio of land to water? What is the ratio of fresh to salt water?
20. How much land is there and how much of it is habitable?
21. Where are the major mountain ranges, oceans, deserts, etc.? Are they consistent with your climates and zones?
22. Have any natural resources been depleted? How and why? Has it caused conflicts?
23. Is the climate hot? Cold? Humid? Rain or snow?
24. What direction does the dominant wind come from? Is it gentle or gale force?

25. Are there seasons? If so, how long and what type are they? Extremes make for extreme changes and can add to a story.
26. Does your climate affect habits of people, such as staying indoors in extremely hot or cold conditions, skiing vs. canoeing.
27. How reliable is the weather from year to year?
28. What catastrophic weather happens? How do people cope?
29. How have human activities affected climate, landforms, etc.? (E.g. The rain forests disappearing from farming.)

Plants and Animals

Once you have your basic background laid out, it's time to add plants and animals. What kinds of trees, flowers, grasses, and so on are there? Take a walk around your neighborhood. Unless you live in a vacuum, there should be some kind of greenery where you live, even if it's nothing more than a tiny weed poking up through the sidewalk. Look at what surrounds you.

Then there are animals. Our world is full of odd and wonderful creatures from minuscule to humongous. The variety is amazing. Be sure your world has as much. Are they: slimy, squishy, exoskeletons, endoskeletons; air breather, water breather, anaerobic, aerobic, likes vacuums; hot blooded, cold blooded, bloodless; blind, sees colors, sees black and white, sees infrared/ultraviolet; hears high/low sounds, thoughts, feels vibrations; good sense of taste; single-celled/multi-celled; bipedal, multi-pedal; furry, scaled, hide, carapace, feathered; reproduces by sex, asexual, buds; is a predator, scavenger, prey; has some defenses; parasitic, symbiotic, sentient; vocal, non-vocal, etc.? These all need to be taken into consideration when making up animals.

Note: while Mr. Spock's parents may have been able to procreate, normally dissimilar species can't. It would be strange for "humans" to have evolved on other planets like we did on Earth, but if this is what you want, be sure you give a reason for it to have happened (seeding?).

While you're thinking of plants, animals, lands, and so on, you'll need names for all of them. We'll get to this more later, but keep things in mind. If you move your humans to new worlds and take cows with them, don't be afraid to use the word "cows". You don't have to dream up weird names for everything. Common ones will work fine.

QUESTIONS:

1. What kind of trees, flowers and other plants are there?
2. Are they sparse or abundant?
3. How do they smell or look?
4. What percent are poisonous or edible?
5. Are any cultivated (grown on purpose)? Are they native or

brought in?

6. What color are the plants?
7. Chlorophyll makes ours green. What chemical colors yours?
8. Plants give us oxygen and we give them CO2. Do your plants and animals co-exist like this?
9. Some plants develop protections. Do yours have any? What are they and why did they develop?
10. Are there animals that can eat the poisonous ones with no problem?
11. What kind of animals live in the different areas?
12. If there are imaginary animals (dragons, etc.), where do they fit into the ecology?
13. What animals, birds, fish, insects are commonly found in which areas? If there are imaginary animals, where do they live?
14. What do they eat? Remember, big animals eat a LOT! If you have a wide variety of big predators, you'll need lots of little animals for them to prey on.
15. Specialists are more efficient, but generalists live longer. Think of koalas or pandas who only eat certain types of greenery. What happens when their food sources die out?
16. If any are intelligent, how does this affect the general ecology? How did they evolve? Do other intelligent species recognize them as intelligent?
17. People take the names of things with them when they go to a new place. What do you call your animals?
18. How do they reproduce? If it's going to be in your story, you need to know.
19. Are there bugs? (There should be). What is their purpose? (Pollination, food, etc.)
20. What do the people and animals eat? Do any plants eat things (like a Venus Flytrap)?
21. Do any animals use tools? What animals? What kind of tools? For what purpose?
22. A lot of Earth plants and animals emit toxins. Some of these toxins are actually useful to humans—if we're careful with them. Do any of your plants or animals have toxic excretions? Are they merely poisonous or can they be used in some way? How?
23. How did your various species evolve?
24. What does it compete with for food, shelter, etc.?

25. What kind of shelter does it need?
26. Live birth or egg or something else?
27. Does it have an impact on the environment?
28. Are they solitary or social? In what way?
29. How long does it live? How old does it have to be to reproduce?
30. How many babies does it have at one time? What does it do—kick them out or nurture them? For how long?
31. What does courtship and mating look like?
32. What is the mortality rate of young?
33. What are its strongest senses? Weakest? Why?
34. What does it have/do to protect itself?
35. Does it have behaviors that are specific to it? (Think of the seahorse where the male holds the young)
36. What are the most prevalent animals? Why?
37. What would happen if they overran the area?
38. Do they carry diseases that can affect the population? What are they and how would one catch them?
39. Don't forget about insects. They play an important part in ecology. Develop them as well.
    a. How big?
    b. How do they look?
    c. Flying? Crawling?
    d. Special effects (like lightning bugs)?
    e. Poisonous? Which ones and in what way?

CHAPTER 2: SOCIETY

You've created the physical aspects of your world, now we need to populate it with people—and I'm not necessarily talking humans here. Remember, the best stories are about conflict. Conflict happens when one person/entity wants something but can't have it because of obstacles that need to be overcome. It doesn't have to be war, it can be something as simple as which way the toilet paper should unroll— though honestly, that is rather lame. It should be something important enough to keep the story moving. It can be personal or global, or even universal, but it should be something the reader can relate to. Three of the most common conflict themes in fiction writing are: man against man, man against himself, man against nature.

In the first, Man against Man, you can have two people arguing over something, or nations or worlds at war. It is the most common type of conflict and occurs in most books.

Man against Himself happens when the main character has inner struggles s/he has to overcome. In this one, think of an alcoholic or drug addict who is trying to get clean and sober. Or someone trying to get over a lost love.

Man against Nature arises when the world itself is causing the problem. Think of a story about a hurricane, volcano, or any disaster story. Or it can be someone lost in the woods in the middle of winter who needs to survive.

Other conflict themes include Man versus Machine as in The Terminator series or 2001: a Space Odyssey. The characters in these stories are fighting against the machines that are trying to control them.

Man versus Society. In this type of conflict, a character must take on society itself, and not a single person. It usually shows up in conspiracy theory stories or post-apocalyptic ones. Or it can be someone like Gandhi or Rosa Parks—someone who stands up for their beliefs no matter the consequences.

Man versus Fate: This conflict is common to fantasy stories where someone has been told his "destiny" is to do something and he fights against it. Think about Harry Potter and how he is fated to not only face Voldemort, but die in order to defeat him. I'd fight against that fate too.

These are types of conflict. So, what kind of conflict will you choose? How will the layout of your physical world work with this conflict? Sometimes the conflicts actually happen over land issues—water rights, mineral rights, boundaries, etc.

In addition, all worlds have a history. It might be a very short history, but it has a history. And that history helps determine what happens in the here and now as well as the future. So... it's history time. And please, no boring the reader. Do make a timeline if you want, with dates and people and important events—that's necessary to keep things straight—but don't write a history book. This is supposed to be interesting.

General Background

QUESTIONS (Note: this is going to get ugly, but bear with me. If you're creating an entire world, you're going to need all this.)

1. What kind of conflict will you choose?
2. Will the lay of the land affect this? In what way?
3. How much of the society you create be involved in this conflict? Will it be two people? Or two million
4. How did this society evolve?
5. Towns and cities
   a. Where are they?
   b. Who founded them?
   c. How were they named? What are their names? Why?
   d. What's the geography/topology of the area? Keep in mind that most human settlements happened near bodies of water for easier transportation, food, water source, etc.
   e. What groups of people live there? In what proportions? Do they congregate in groups of similar beings?
   f. Where do the most prestigious people live? What about the lower castes/classes?
   g. Are there different shopping districts for the different classes? Why? What happens if someone goes to a

different class area for shopping?

    h. Are there areas where crooks tend to congregate? Why?

    i. Are there areas where there is gambling, prostitution, drugs, etc.? Are these allowed? If not, who polices them and what happens?

    j. Are there areas of manufacturing? What kinds? Where do the workers live? Why?

    k. Is the town/city stable? How long has it existed?

    l. Who is in charge of running the town/city? (Mayor, Lord, King, Dictator, etc.)

    m. Are there areas where there is entertainment? What kind? Who is allowed to go?

    n. Are there parks or central areas for gatherings?

    o. Are there museums? Who is allowed in? What do they display? What about libraries?

    p. Are there festivals or holidays central to this area? What ones? Why are they celebrated? How did they start?

    q. Are there foods specific to this area? What are they?

    r. Are there sports teams? What kinds?

    s. Where are the oldest buildings? The newest? Towns are not static. They are always changing, so should yours. Who built the town? Why?

6. How far back are there records of historical events and how well known are the stories?

7. Do people believe the records or take them as stories that may or may not be based on fact?

8. Are there manmade (being-made) landmarks or only natural ones?

    a. Where and what are they?

    b. Why are they important?

    c. Who made them (if constructed) and how?

9. How long have people been in this world? Did they evolve or arrive? How and from where did they arrive? Why did they come there?

10. If non-human sentient or magical beings, where did they come from?

11. Where did civilization begin? How did it spread? How was its development helped or hindered by the presence of non-humans (either magic or alien life).

12. Which people/countries are the most advanced technologically? Least advanced? What kinds of problems does this difference cause? (man vs. man)
13. How accessible is this country? What natural features mark the borders? Who are the neighboring countries and how do they get along? Why did the people settle in this area in the first place (strategic location, trade route, water, minerals, farming, etc.) Have things changed much since then?
14. If this is an alternate universe, is there a specific point in history where this world split off from ours? (e.g. Napoleon won at Waterloo)? If so, what was it? How much has changed and will continue to change as a result? What caused the split?
15. If there is no point of divergence, what are the differences between this world and ours? (See magic section for more questions on this area.)
16. How do the weapons of this country compare with those of surrounding area? What major weapons of war are available?
17. Who are the heroes and villains of the history (Lincoln, Washington, J. Wilkes Booth, Benedict Arnold) Why are they heroes/villains?
18. How large is the population and what are the types (urban, rural, etc.)? How does it compare with other countries and the world in general?
19. Is the population mobile (nomadic or moves a lot)? Are they shifting to other areas in general (drought, flooding, volcanoes)? Why? Where are they going?
20. Is there much immigration/emigration? From or to where? Why?
21. How diverse is the population? Are there minorities? What are the percentages?
22. Are rural areas mostly farms, forests, grazing fields or waste land?

People

You need people to populate your world. For science fiction, they can be human or alien, but they still have to be able to live on your planet. For historical, remember that ancient Norse were different than modern Scandinavians. Our ancestors were shorter than we are today. Their languages were different as were their clothes.

A. Physical – general
1. Size (height, weight, build)
2. Coloring (hair, skin, eyes)
3. Uniqueness – what is special about this people as a whole?
B. Language
1. Do they speak a language all their own or is it a mixture of multiple languages?
2. Do some peoples have non-verbal languages? (hand signals, tweeting like birds, clicking sounds, etc.)
3. Is there a general language for all classes and cultures and a specific one for each ethnic group?
4. How many languages are there? Which ones are related? Do they borrow words from each other?
5. Is there a trade language that facilitates commerce between countries that don't speak the same language?
6. Are some or all people bilingual?
7. What are the variations in speech patterns, syntax and slang from one social class to another? Does it vary by occupation? Region? Race?
8. What areas do local slang phrases come out of? (in a fishing town, a good catch can mean a bountiful catch but farmers would call it a good harvest)
9. What things would this culture have many specific words for? (Inuit languages have fourteen words for snow)
10. Are there words that must never be spoken except at particular times/ceremonies/circumstances? Words that must never be spoken?
11. What will people swear a binding oath by?
12. What are curse words? Who uses them? When?
13. Is there a written alphabet? What does it look like? What does it sound like?
14. Is there a single accepted calendar? If not, how do different ones meld with others?
15. Is there a single time calculation? How do people tell time? How is the day broken up into smaller time units? Is the length of time fixed or determined by the length of daylight? How do they get up in the morning? (sunrise,

bells)

16. What are the names of days, months? How many in each? What events do they use to date years? (End of the great war? Creation of the world?)

C. Family

1. What is a normal family unit?
2. How extended is an extended family?
3. How important are family connections?
4. What is their attitude toward handicapped or disabled people? Are they treated with respect? Ignored? Or killed so as to better the species?

D. Costume—clothing can be determined by climate, general landscape, people's beliefs, and more. It can be prim or exaggeratedly ridiculous. Colors can be muted or wild.

1. Is it plain or colorful?
2. Does it differ by class, occupation, age or gender?
3. How expensive is it?
4. Can the material be produced locally?
5. Are certain clothes customary for certain occupations (uniforms, robes, etc.).
6. Are certain colors reserved for certain classes? Are there laws defining who can wear what?
7. How many times a day/week/year do they change clothes? How do they keep them clean?
8. What materials and styles are common to the climate? Are some styles appropriate for one country but not another?
9. Does any group dress differently from anyone else? (rebellious youngsters) If so, how is it looked upon?
10. Weaponry – who carries it? What do they carry? Is it used for personal protection or by law keepers? Are there special clothing adaptations for it (to keep hidden or belts with loops, etc.) Are personal weapons available to anyone who can afford them?
11. How much do non-human fashions reflect their physiology?

CHAPTER 3: GOVERNMENT

Government

All societies have governments, even if they're very loosely based. Even animals have a sort of hierarchy within the different species, usually the strongest animal is the leader. The banding together of like peoples is often determined by the lay of the land (who lives where) which determines the type of society and government there will be. The following questions will help you build your society.

Social Rankings - Royalty or ruling class – this has a lot to do with the political structure. Generally speaking, a democracy does not have royalty (Great Britain is an example of a monarchy/democracy).

QUESTIONS:

1. How they treat others is important. Are they greedy? Benevolent?
2. How difficult is it to move from one social level to another? How is advancement done (marriage, money, ruler gift)? How much resistance is there from those already in that class?
3. What classes do you have?
    a. Ruling class – these are the people at the top of the food chain.
    b. Commercial class – these are the merchants, shopkeepers, solid middle class people – do you have a commercial class?
    c. Commoners, workers – the people who get their hands dirty for pay. The underlings, but not slave class. Who are your commoners/workers?
    d. Slave class (if any) – people who are forced to work for no pay. Again, if your society has a slave class, their treatment is a marker as to what type of society they are.
    e. Scholars, religious leaders, lawyers – another middle class, but not merchants. These are generally people who are higher on the class list than commoners, but

may actually be poorer than them. Their step on the class ladder is determined by their importance in your society. The more the society reveres education, religion and laws, the higher they'll be.

f. Military — if any. Do they come from all layers of society or mainly one over the other? How is rank determined? Can any soldier advance in rank or only elite? Is it open to both (or all) genders? Where do they fit in class society? How old are those who join? Can one retire (leave) the service without the excuse of major injury? How and what are they taught?

Politics

Every society has a political structure, even if it seems like it doesn't. Politics figure heavily into the way your characters live their lives (and you live yours). Think about the differences between how Americans live vs. the Chinese. Big differences—and all because of politics. Your language, dress, work, freedoms—all of it depends on the politics of the land. Think about your countries and the people who populate those areas. How do the politics of their land affect them? What about other lands?

QUESTIONS:

1. What is the structure of the society: matriarch, patriarch, bureaucracy, federation, empire, republic, etc.?
2. Is it based on city states, or other political boundaries?
3. Who levies taxes? For what? How are the collectors paid? How are the taxes paid? (money or crops, etc.)
4. Who can give orders to army, tax collectors, servants, etc.? How are they chosen?
5. If an electoral system, who may vote? Is age a factor? Race? Gender?
6. How much influence do special groups have on government? Is it overt or under the table? Is bribery an accepted practice?
7. What are the controversial issues facing the government?

8. Who makes the laws? Who carries out the laws?

9. Who pays the crook-catcher (cops/guards/etc.) (government, merchants, etc.)?

10. How are they organized? Are they full-time/part-time, volunteers? Public or private?

11. Are there enough law enforcement personnel to do their job? How are they paid? What is the level of corruption?

12. Where do judges, lawyers, police fit into society? Are they revered or reviled? How are they trained? Paid? What do they wear?

13. What are considered normal and legal ways of gathering evidence and determining guilt? Is torture allowed? How are prisoners treated before and after conviction?

14. Are people presumed innocent until proven guilty?

15. Are there separate civil and criminal courts?

16. What things are considered truly serious crimes and why? What are punishments for serious and minor crimes?

17. Are there prisons? What do they look like? How are they governed?

18. Are there degrees of punishment (cutting off body part? Branding? Jail?) Are appeals allowed?

19. Are highwaymen, pirates, muggers common or rare? What sort of crimes are common?

20. How is justice handled in outlying areas? Is Mob Rule tolerated?

21. Are there classes or people with fewer legal rights? Why?

22. If laws are different in different countries, what happens if something is illegal in one country but legal in another? Does this cause problems?

23. Relations with others—are they warlike or peaceful? How do they handle conflict with others?

24. Which people/countries/races have traditionally fought, allied, traded or been rivals? Where are there still hard feelings? Are there still hard feelings about old events? (feuds)

25. Who can be an ambassador? How are treaties arranged? Are there standing embassies or envoys only when there is a problem?

26. How do official attitudes affect trade?
27. Is there formal spying (CIA)? By whom and for what? (merchants, rulers, scientists, etc.) Are any heads of state related to others through marriage? How does this affect relations? What does the government provide? (schools, medicine, food) On a local or general basis? How is equity determined – or isn't it?
28. Who is considered a citizen? How do you become a citizen? Can you advance in social status? How? What kinds of people are likely to face prejudice?
29. Who protects the head of state? Who takes over is something happens to him/her?
30. Is there any organized crime? Who runs it?
31. Who is in charge of fighting crime? How are they organized?
32. Are there silly laws that nobody follows but are still there?
33. How corrupt is the government? Is anything done to curb it?

Military and war

With politics comes military and wars. Governments that are trying to keep their space theirs, or are trying to usurp other areas, go to war. So they need militaries/guards/knights to fight for them. So you need to figure them out.

QUESTIONS:

1. How are armies structured?
2. Are battlefield commissions possible?
3. Who can call up men for an army and how? Are there professional soldiers/mercenaries? How large is a typical army? How are they supplied?
4. What happens if the supply is cut off? How many days' worth of supplies can be carried? Is the army integrated? (women, non-humans, classes all together)
5. How is war waged? (only fight in winter when nobody is busy with farming; can't make war on civilians; can only use certain

weapons).

6. Who handles things back home during long campaigns?
7. What is the level of weapons technology?
8. If there is magic, is it used in war? In what way? By whom?
9. Are magical weapons available?
10. Can magic make weapons more effective?
11. Do you have to do anything special to walls, armor or weapons to make them better able to resist enemy spells?
12. How much does the presence of magic affect strategy?
13. Is magic primarily used for spying or directly on the battlefield?
14. How can it be defended against?
15. If non-humans, are they adept at particular weapons? Why? (strength, sight, etc.)
16. If a long-term war is in progress, how has the home front been affected? Are people being drafted much younger/older than before? Have people been forced to take over unusual jobs (Rosie the Riveter); how has this affected society?
17. Are there natural or imposed limitations prohibiting the development or use of certain types of weapons? What are they and why?
18. What weapons and armor are standard for armies? Mercenaries? Nobility? Peasants defending their homes?
19. What was the biggest war in history? Why did it start? How did it end (if it did). If not, why not?

CHAPTER 4: ECONOMY

Money System

Any society needs a system of trade/money. It can be as simple as seashells or beads, or as complicated as minted money with specific denominations. Or maybe a barter system—but even that requires rules.

QUESTIONS:

1. What kind of money do they use or is it barter based?
2. If monetary, is it minted, printed or both? What does it look like? What is it made of? What are the values? Who determines the values? Who mints it? How easy is it to counterfeit? (Note: if you decide that coins are 1/10 of an ounce and you have to pay a large ransom, it can get really heavy if you don't have paper money.)
3. What is it called?
4. If you have more than one country, can money from one be used in another?
5. If barter based, who or what determines the value of goods and services? Are they consistent across towns/countries?
6. What types of currency is a traveler or merchant likely to carry?
7. Is currency standardized or is there a system of exchange?
8. Are there taxes? What kind and who levies them and how are they collected? What are they used for?

Commerce

This goes hand-in-hand with money. People need a way to get goods. Very few people are completely self-sufficient/contained. Everybody needs something from someone. So… where do they get the goods/services they need?

QUESTIONS:

1. Do they have free trade with other countries?
2. Do they have to import a lot of their goods or export a lot?
3. What do they have of value to other societies?
4. What do they import/export?
5. Are imports/exports regulated by government/guilds/cartels? How does this affect relations?
6. Are there customs inspections at the borders?
7. If they are a closed society, how do they get things they don't have but need?
8. Are there trade unions? Do any of them transcend borders?
9. Are people able to learn or perform different trades? Does cross training require permission? From whom? What types of trades would there be in small towns vs. large cities?
10. Are industrial processes (weaving, sword-making, etc.) trade secrets or common knowledge?
11. How does a person enter a craft or trade? (apprenticeship? School? Internship?) Are people able to cross-craft? Does this require guild or government permission? How strict are craft guilds? (can only carpenters build houses).
12. Do different regions specialize in different crafts? (Chinese silk, Bordeaux wine, etc.)
13. What types of trades would be represented in small towns vs. large cities?
14. How is business organized? Are there trade unions? Corporations? Cartels?
15. What regulations, if any, do the rulers have? (anti-monopoly? Anti-pollution? Standardized systems of weights and measurement?)
16. How are records kept? (tally sticks, books, beads) and who keeps them? Are they standardized? By whom?
17. What industries (mining, fishing, shipbuilding, lumber, etc.) are important and where?
18. What are considered luxury items? (Chocolate? Coffee, silk, paper, etc.)

Agriculture

All countries have to have some sort of agriculture going on. Whether plant or animal based, there will be a need by everyone for food. Yes, there can be hunters/gatherers. But even this is "agriculture". In some societies, it may be cooperatives with people coming together to provide for the entire town; or in others, there may be individual family farms; or even huge conglomerates that provide for large areas. Everyone needs food—how do they get it?

QUESTIONS:

1. Is there any farming? If so, what kind?
2. What are their prevalent crops, farm animals? What animals are used for food and for work? Can work animals be used for food?
3. Are the farms family owned, feudal or cooperatives (goes back to the type of political system they have)?
4. Are rural areas primarily farms, forests, grazing, or waste land?
5. How much food is it possible to ship before it spoils? (state of roads in rural areas)
6. What is the growing season like? (see weather/climate). What crops cannot be grown because of soil, climate, etc. Are any crops grown strictly for export? (drugs?)
7. Are any wild animals available for use (fir, whale oil, feathers, etc.) or are some taboo?
8. If no agriculture, how do they get their food? Are they hunter/gatherers?
9. Are there laws in place to protect animals from extinction? If so, who controls them and what are the guidelines?
10. What is considered valuable in this culture (gold, jewels, drugs, money, land, etc.) Why? Do different races value different things? Is there a race that values non-material things (info, time)?

Food
1. Where does it come from?
2. Are there foods that are unique to this ethnic society (whether by choice or as determined by their geography)? Is it spicy,

bland, sweet? What is drunk (water, milk, wine, beer, cider)? What are staples?

3. Does one ingredient seem indigenous to the group (as rice is to Asian, corn to central America, wheat to North America, coconut to the islands, etc.)

4. Do men, women, parents/children, master/peasant eat together or separately? How is status displayed at the table (above the salt)

5. What dishes are considered holiday food? Foods for events (weddings, funerals, etc.), times of year (turkey)?

6. What distinguishes a formal dinner from an everyday meal? How do court manners differ from others?

7. What eating utensils are used?

8. What is the order of a typical meal for each class? (wine, sweet, stew, salad, meat – or all at once)? Who is served first?

9. How many meals are eaten in a typical day?

10. Are special arrangements made for visitors (higher chairs for dwarves, raw meat for werewolves, perches for harpies, etc.)

11. Is sanitation good enough to make untreated water safe? What else do people drink?

12. How is food preserved? How reliable are the methods? If food is limited, who eats first? Why?

13. What shapes are tables? Where is the place of honor for a guest?

14. What things, while edible, are never eaten? Why? Are some common foods poisonous to other species?

15. What do things smell like? Taste like?.

CHAPTER 5: LIFE IN GENERAL

Education

1. Is there any and is it available for all people or only the elite or one sex over the other? How far can they go? How much does it cost?
2. What things are considered necessary knowledge for different levels or classes? Which would be embarrassing if discovered (passion for poetry by warrior)?
3. Is it valued? Is it government controlled or open (politicians say what can and cannot be taught)?
4. Is it done at home, at school or other gathering place? Who teaches?
5. Who are the teachers and how are they trained? Who pays them?
6. What is the level of literacy of the general population?
7. What things are considered necessary knowledge for different sects?
8. Where is research done and how is it funded? Private or government?
9. Where do students come from and how old are they?
10. What does the school year look like?
11. Do different beings attend the same schools? Why not?
12. What kinds of schools are there? Elementary? High school? College?
13. Are the schools boarding schools? Where do students stay? Teachers?
14. Are there activities beyond learning? What kind?
15. What subjects do they learn?
16. Are there rivalries between schools? Why and what kind?
17. What do teachers do when they're not teaching?
18. Is there security at the school?
19. Are there ways around security? How do the kids sneak out?
20. Are there punishments? What kind and for what?
21. Are there things prohibited on school grounds?
22. Do the schools provide food? Is it any good?

23. Is there a dress code? What is it?
24. What kinds of supplies do the students need? Who provides them? What if the students can't afford them?
25. Is there a "scholarship" program for poor students?
26. Who founded the school and why? Did anyone famous go there? Who?
27. Has the school changed over the years? In what way?
28. How is the head of the school chosen?
29. Are there different schools for different subjects? (Magic, science, medicine, arts, music, woodworking, technology, etc.)

Customs

1. What are the rites of passage? (formalized ritual or informal), different for men and women? For nobility and peasants?
2. How is marriage conducted?
3. Do partners get to choose or are they arranged?
4. Who performs the marriage rite?
5. What are the marriage customs?
6. Are there special ceremonies/foods/clothing?
7. What about the marriage night—is there a honeymoon phase?
8. Is marriage civil or religious?
9. What are courtship customs?
10. Is there divorce? If so, what happens to dissolve a marriage? Are there any ramifications for the person left? What about the person leaving?
11. What customs surround birth? Is the mother sequestered? Formal presentation to family/society? Are men involved in birth? Is there birth control?
12. How are names given?
13. How do they treat children – as gifts or commodities? Are children raised in family units or crèches? Is reproduction celebrated or hidden? Is there a ceremony at birth, naming day, coming of age, etc.?
14. Who raises the children? At what age do they begin to be educated and trained? By whom?
15. What things are considered shocking in this society (showing a woman's ankle, eating left-handed)? What would the reaction be if someone saw this happening? Are there words that are

taboo? Why?

16. What are social taboos? (wearing bathing suit to office) What are consequences?
17. What are the acceptable limits to honor and/or honesty? Are white lies acceptable? Is thievery an accepted, if disreputable, occupation or crime?
18. Is a binding oath unbreakable no matter what? Does it pass to the heirs? What if two oaths conflict?
19. What are the attitudes toward ownership? What can be stolen?
20. Who is considered a citizen? Who grants citizenship?
21. What are controversial subjects in this culture? What would start a friendly argument? What would start a major fight?
22. What are social faux pas? (burping? Drawing steel in presence of royalty? Asking what sex another species is?)
23. What sports or games are there? What is their importance in society? Are there rules that need to be written up? Who can play?
24. What job skills are considered the most important? Why? Which are least useful? Why? Are special skills needed for any of these? How do the workers get the training for them?
25. What are the standards of beauty for people? Art? Clothing? Furnishings? How are they different between cultures/species?
26. What kinds of people are the rebels and outcasts of this society? How does society deal with them? (special living conditions, ignored, invisible)
27. Who are the social heroes? (Mother Theresa)
28. What are standards of personal hygiene?
29. How are garbage and other waste materials disposed of?
30. Is there plumbing? Who builds and maintains? How reliable are they? How do they differ from one area to the next? Indoor or outdoor?

Charitable foundations

1. Are there any?
2. Who runs them?
3. How are they funded?
4. Who benefits?

5. If none, what happens to the poor or in emergencies?

Manners

1. How do they act toward one another within the family? Within their social group? With neighbors? With outsiders? With other countries?
2. Are social mores strict or relaxed? Do they differ between classes and sexes? How do they treat those with different mores?
3. When meeting someone, how are they greeted (handshake, bow, etc.) How did the gesture originate? Is there a special greeting for select groups/sexes/castes/etc.
4. What are the polite forms of address? (my lord, my lady, your holiness, etc.)
5. Is there a way to make a greeting insulting?
6. How are two strangers introduced? Who gets introduced first? (sex/class/race)
7. Are there classes who are never introduced (pariahs?)
8. Are true names given or hidden from some people?
9. Are there occupations that are reviled? Revered?
10. Are full names/titles given or just a short form? (nicknames)
11. How are friends seen at a distance acknowledged (smile and wave)? What is a comfortable polite speaking distance?
12. Are gestures and body language subtle or not? Do people talk with their hands or is that vulgar?
13. What gestures are insulting or have different meanings between different cultures?
14. How do you show respect to superiors (bow, salute, etc.)
15. Are there questions which must be avoided (how much money you make, politics, religion, etc.)
16. How serious does society take rules of visitation? How and when are you considered a host (in Mid-east, giving bread and salt to someone makes them your guest; serving them a huge meal but no bread or salt doesn't)
17. What is polite to offer (food, drink, bed, entertainment,

personal staff, guards, sex)?

18. What is it rude to refuse or not ask for?
19. When a guest arrives, are food and drink offered immediately or only on request? Or after a short time? Is there a particular food or drink that is customary to offer?

Religion

1. Deity – Is the deity a male or female – or multiple? What is/are s/he/they named? Is/Are s/he/they kind and benevolent or malevolent? If multiple, what does each rule over? Is the deity real (corporeal) or spiritual?
2. If corporeal, is there rivalry between the gods? How does it affect religion and the people? Are they interested in the people? Why or why not?
3. Can the deity be killed?
4. Do they require sacrifices? What kinds?
5. How do you become a follower? A priest?
6. Can all races, sexes, etc. practice and become a head?
7. Is there an afterlife? What's it like?
8. Are the deities responsible for creating anything? What?
9. What is sacred to each deity? Why?
10. Are any places sacred? Why? Where?
11. Do the deities have families? Who? What is the relationship? Religious observances, rites, holidays – are there special holy days? If so, for what?
12. Who or what does the holiday celebrate? Why?
13. How popular is this holiday?
14. How is it observed? Special foods? Fasts? Number of days?
15. How important is it?
16. Is it a fun one? Or serious? Why?
17. Is there music? What kind? Instrumental or vocal? Who may sing?
18. Are there special symbols associated with this holiday? What? And what does it mean?
19. Are there decorations associated with it? What kinds?
20. Is there special clothing people wear because of this holiday? What and why?
21. Are there superstitions associated with this holiday? What are

they and why do they exist? What happens if you break one?

22. What kinds of ceremonies, if any, are held for births, deaths, marriages and other special occasions?
23. Are there different levels of religion for the different classes?
24. Are there times when fasting or feasting is required? Who provides the feast?
25. Holy books, icons – are there religious books, symbols or other icons specific to the deity? Are they available to all members of society or only certain people (religious leaders, elite, men, etc.)
26. Where does the church fit in society? Is it a state church or different sects? Is there freedom of religion?
27. How much of a part does religion play in public and private life?
28. How do people decide who to worship? What offerings are acceptable?
29. Do people see the church as a good thing or a parasite?
30. Who sets the moral/ethical codes? Why?
31. Which ethical decisions are social, which are religious?
32. Are priests full-time or do they need other jobs?
33. How is evil explained? (Satan/devil/evil god)
34. Is there a difference between magic and miracles? What?
35. How do religions view magic/non-humans?
36. Do any religions require or forbid magic?

Folklore

1. What are the myths, legends, superstitions, etc. of the people?
2. Do they pass stories down from one generation to the next?
3. Are stories verbal or written down?
4. How were they developed? Most myths exist to explain the unexplainable.
5. Do any of the stories affect social mores, rites, religions?
6. Are there differences between peoples and stories that cause conflict? (One group believes a legend as a hero, another sees him as a villain).

Death

1. How do they handle death? Are there ceremonies, specific rites, or preparations?
2. Is euthanasia an acceptable alternative to pain and suffering? How do they treat those who are nearing the end – with dignity or by ignoring them?
3. What of suicides – are they treated differently?
4. How are the families of the deceased treated?
5. How is inheritance handled?
6. What happens to the belongings of the deceased? What if there is no family?
7. Who deals with the body? What must be done and why? (Burn to free the spirit, bury, coins on eyes, belongings)
8. Are the dead feared, revered, ignored?

CHAPTER 6: THE ARTS AND SCIENCES

Every society has art and science. It may be something as simple as weaving cloth for clothes or using herbs for healing. Or it can be complicated. You need to decide. But remember this, there are no absolutes. Science can be art and art is science. Music has mathematical basics in the notes. Colors used for weaving an painting are based on three primary colors. Everything else is a combination of these three—and all can be broken down into wavelengths on the color spectrum. Both science and art are necessary for each other.

QUESTIONS:

Arts (Literature, music, fine arts, textiles, etc.)

1. Does the society place any value on the arts?
2. Can anyone participate or is it elitist?
3. Are the artists supported or live from hand to mouth?
4. Are the arts appreciated or disdained?
5. Is there music? Musical instruments? Who can play? What are they like?
6. Are there permanent theaters? Who owns and runs them? Are there traveling troupes?
7. What do different classes do for fun?
    a. What sports or pastimes are common? (hawking, hunting, skiing, ball games, etc.)
    b. Which ones take money, skill, or too much time?
    c. What games are commonly known (chess, dice, cards). Can anyone play?
    d. Are certain societies known for a particular skill?
8. Have paper-making, printing presses been invented?
9. Are there libraries? Who has access?
10. Are there subjects that are taboo for the arts?
11. Can magic be used in the arts? How? (instruments that play themselves)
12. Are there non-human races who tend to be naturally talented in certain arts? What and why?
13. Do non-humans have their own games/sports/pastimes?
14. How are messages sent when necessary? Postal system (public

or private?) How fast is it? How do people get news of the world (town crier? Newspaper)

15. How are books produced? Is there censorship? By whom?
16. Are there libraries? Where? Are they available to all? Who supports them?

Medicine and other sciences

1. Are there doctors, hospitals, medical centers? Or are people seen at their homes?
2. Is the medicine science based (chemical drugs) or lore based (herbs, superstition, etc.).
3. Is it modern by our standards or sub-par?
4. Is it available to all or only those who can pay?
5. Who diagnoses and treats? What is their education?
6. How accurate is diagnosis?
7. How much is known about anatomy, physiology, pathology, etc.?
8. Where do healers learn their arts? If magic, does the healer have to consciously direct the process or does magic simply speed up healing? Is there more than one kind of magical healer?
9. Are there both magical and non-magical healers? Who uses which and why? Are they rivals?
10. What is the mortality rate for birth? Other diseases?
11. Is it possible to resurrect someone who has died? How long after death is this possible?
12. How is insanity treated? Are there asylums or treatment centers? How effective are treatments? What about other mental illnesses like depression?
13. How much do physical differences between humans and non-humans affect treatment? Are there diseases that affect only one or the other? Are some treatments lethal to one group but good for another? Are there separate doctors for each species?
14. Are other sciences tolerated or frowned upon?
15. What happens to a scientist who proposes a new idea that is contrary to popular opinion?
16. Where is research done? How is it supported? (corporate, private, public)

17. What kind of technology do they have?
18. Does the level of technological advancement match the level of social and political advancement?
19. Technology solves a problem. What problem does the technology of your world solve? Why is it there? Who made it and how?
20. What important inventions have been made (gunpowder, flush toilets, printing press)? Do they affect the daily lives of average person?
21. What kind of tools do they use?
22. What inventions have not been made – for this level of society?
23. Who can use technology? I know what an x-ray machine is but I don't know how to use one.
24. Do people fear new technology? Or are they trying to improve what they have and find new ways to use it?
25. How much is known about the laws of nature, physics and magic? How much knowledge is wrong? (world is flat, sun revolves around earth)
26. In what areas might magic replace technology, perhaps suppressing its development (spell to keep food cold is easy so refrigerators not needed)?

CHAPTER 7: HOUSING AND TRANSPORTATION

Once you have people, you need places for them to live and ways for them to get around. Do they live in caves? Or large cities? Or something in between? Castles or huts? Walk or use personal flying devices?

QUESTIONS:

Housing

1. What does it look like? How is it shaped? (domed, square, hexagons)
2. Where is it? (underground, above ground, in the trees? In caves?)
3. Is it single family or collective dwellings? What kinds of rooms are there? How big?
4. What is it constructed of?
    a. How available are construction materials?
    b. What is the most common material?
    c. Is there a material not used for a reason? Why? (wood – too flammable)
5. Who builds? How is it built?
6. How is it lighted, heated, cooled, accessed?
7. Is there indoor plumbing? If not, what alternatives are there for waste?
8. What are the differences between ruling class and lower class dwellings?
9. What do typical floor plans look like? Can people afford to waste space on halls or does one room open into another?
10. How many people live in a typical house? How are living quarters arranged? (bedrooms on top for privacy or ground floor for convenience)
11. Are parlors or libraries common?
12. How tall can a building be? Does war affect types of housing?
13. How are buildings decorated? (paint, carvings, tile)

Cities
1. How are cities/towns laid out—grid or haphazard?
2. Is the center of government at the center of the city?
3. Are there public or private parks? Who takes care of them?
4. How wide are streets/alleys? Is there a reason?
5. What are the landmarks? Where are the interesting neighborhoods? The bad side of town?
6. Where do people go to shop/eat/have fun? Is there a tourist area?
7. What sorts of foods/entertainment/housing is available? Is it different for smaller towns?
8. What is available in cities that is not in villages?
9. Are peasants tied to their land or can they move to town?
10. Do non-humans and humans live in the same towns? On the same street? Or is there segregation? By law or by social standards?

Transportation

1. How do they get around? By foot? Horse or other animal? Cart? Auto? Mass transportation? Trains, boats, planes, jets, spaceships?
2. What is the cost of transportation?
3. Is it available to all?
4. What is the fastest method? Safest? Do they hop/fly/swim/run/bounce/slither/float…?
5. How available is water transportation? How reliable? How dangerous? How expensive?
6. Are there differences for short distance vs. long distance?
7. Do some classes not travel without permission? (slaves)
8. Where do travelers stay? Do some classes never travel? Do some always travel (nomads, gypsies)?
9. Is there such a thing as traveling for "fun" (vacation)?
10. Is magical or advanced technical transportation available? What type? Is it regulated? By whom and how?
11. If there are crafts, what does they run on?
    a. How easy is it to refuel?
    b. Where do you get the fuel?
    c. How does it move?

12. How large are your crafts? If there is a large crew, you'll need quarters, food, etc. for them.
    a. If you have a crew, where do they sleep?
    b. What do they eat and where do you store it?
    c. How do you prevent crankiness from being stuck in a ship for long periods of time?
    d. How do you keep them healthy?
    e. What do you do to repair damage?
    f. Where can you land or dock?
13. If a spaceship, how do you handle gravity?
    a. What about "wormholes" or other things needed for traversing huge distances between planets without the characters dying of old age?
    b. Are they generational ships?
    c. How do you deal with waste management?
    d. What about air?
    e. What do you do about power failures?
    f. Are there weapons? What kind? Why?
    g. Where is it built? In space, or on a planet?

CHAPTER 8: FANTASY AND SCIENCE FICTION

Fantasy Elements

If you're creating a fantasy or science fiction universe, you need specialty items that don't occur in the normal world. These can affect all aspects of your world—from governments to societies to arts and transportation. Do people use magic every day? Or fly dragons? Or mind-speak with each other? This next section will help you flesh out your fantasy or science fiction elements.

QUESTIONS:

Geography and History

1. If there are non-human inhabitants, are there any areas they claim as their own? (e.g. dwarves usually live underground)
2. How does Magic fit in to this world?
3. How do magical beasts fit in?
4. How similar are the history and culture of the magic realm to the non-magic realm? Why is it so similar/different?
5. If magic is known to exist, which historical events have changed and which are the same?
6. If magic exists but history is the same, why has it had no effect?
7. If magic exists but nobody knows about it, why and how has it been kept secret?
8. How numerous are the magic creatures? Where do they live? What do they eat? How much habitat do they require? Are they intelligent?

Magic and Magicians

1. What things can magic NOT do? What are the limits to magical power? How do magicians try to get around these limits?
2. What is the price magicians must pay in order to be magicians? Years of study, permanent celibacy, using up bits of their life or memory with each spell, etc.? Does anyone ever try to get around the price of magic?

3. Is there a difference between miracles and magic? If so, how are they distinguished?
4. Where does magic power come from? The gods, the mana or the world, the personal willpower of the magician? Is it an exhaustible resource? If the magician must feed his spells with his own willpower, what long-term effects will this have on the health and/or stability of the magician?
5. Do different races/species/genders have different sources for their magic?
6. How does a magician tap into his source of power?
7. Does becoming a magician require some rite of passage (being chosen by the gods, given a link to the source) or does it just happen naturally as a gradual result of study or as part of growing up?
8. What do you need to do to cast a spell – design a ritual, recite poetry, mix the right ingredients in a pot?
9. Are there things like a staff, wand, familiar, crystal ball that are necessary to have before casting a spell? Whe
10. Where do new wizards get these things? Do they make them, buy them, inherit them or find them?
11. Is there a limit to the number of wizards in the world? Why? What is it?
12. How long does it take to cast a spell? Can they be stored for later, instant use? Does working them take a lot of long ritual time or is it a "point and shoot" affair?
13. Can two or more wizards combine their power to cast a stronger spell or is it an individual thing?
14. What makes one wizard more powerful than another? (having a knowledge of more spells, ability to handle greater levels of power, having a more powerful patron, etc.)
15. Are certain spells/rituals illegal? Why? What are the consequences? How are they detected? How are they punished? By whom?
16. Does practicing magic have any detrimental effect on the magician (addictive, insanity, shortening life-span)? Is there any way to prevent the effect? Are the effects inevitable to all magicians or do they affect only certain ones? Do they progress at the same rate in everyone? Are they universal in all species or are some races (dwarves, elves, etc.) immune to them?

17. How much is known about the laws of nature, physics and magic?
18. What general varieties of magic are practiced (herbal potions, rituals, alchemy, demonology, necromancy, etc.)? Do any work better than others or does only one variety work at a time?
19. Are certain kinds of magic practiced solely by one sex/race or the other? Is this because of inborn ability, natural preference or legislation?
20. Does a magician's power change over time? (growing stronger or weaker during puberty or with increasing age?) Can a magician use up all of his magic? If so, what happens to the ex-mage (dies, retires, teaches, consults)?
21. Can the ability to do magic be lost? If so, how (burn out? Illness?)
22. Can the ability be taken away? If so, how and by whom? (if only a virgin can work spells, sex will take the ability away)
23. What is the price magicians must pay in order to be magicians (years of study, permanent celibacy, using up bits of their life or memory with each spell)? Does anyone ever get around the price?
24. How do various religions view magic? Do any forbid it? Why or why not? Do any require it? Who performs (priests/priestesses)
25. How long does it take to learn? Where do you go to learn it? School or mentors? Is an untrained wizard dangerous? How do they fund their training?
26. Is it a profession, an art or just a job? What social status do magicians hold? Are they admired or reviled?
27. Can anyone become a wizard or do you have to be born that way?
28. Are they organized? How? What happens if the top person dies? Who takes over? How is it determined?
29. Are different races/species good at different types of magic? If so, what types are associated with what races/species? Are there ones that use magic more or less unconsciously (dragons who use magic to fly without thinking about it)
30. Can you make a living practicing magic or do you have to be rich? What's a wizard's job market like? What's their income like compared to the rest of society?
31. Are wizards a force in politics or are they above it? Do they

have a lobby? Do they need one? (others trying to outlaw, protect or promote certain kinds, licensing, etc.)

32. Are licenses needed? What kind? (like a driver's license or doctor's?) who certifies?
33. How do locals view them? Are they good guys, bad guys, called in only in emergencies, regular working stiffs, ivory tower academics, nuisances, dangerous, etc.
34. Are they barred from certain kinds of government jobs or offices? Do some jobs require it?
35. Do they have a special language that is used for magic? Where do they learn it? Is it safe to chat in this language or is everything automatically a spell?
36. Is magic considered a science or are scientists and magicians enemies? Are the two compatible? To what degree does magic replace or supplement technology?
37. Is the power of a country relative to the number or power of wizards there?
38. Are there magical means of transportation? How do they compare to non-magical means (speed, safety, comfort)? How often are they used and for what purposes?
39. Are magical weapons available? Has the presence of magic affected weapons technology? Can magic make them more or less effective? Can an ordinary object be enchanted to make it a lethal weapon?
40. Can spells or magical items be mass-produced? Can businesses use magicians to be more efficient/successful? Can they use magic to ruin other businesses?

Science Fiction

1. If you've created an alien, how are they similar to humans?
2. How are they different?
3. If different, how do they breathe? Move? Procreate? Eat?
4. What is their structure?
5. What is their basic building block? (Copper, silicon, etc.)
6. Warm-blooded or cold-blooded?
7. How many senses? (Not all animals have five.)
8. What is their culture like? (Note: you might want to go through the government/social sections above for your alien

species).
9. How do they communicate (talk)?
10. Are they more or less advanced than humans?

CHAPTER 9: THE END

YOU'RE DONE!

If you've gone through this all, by now, you have an amazing world that is completely your own creation. That's a lot of work, but it's worth it. You will probably never use even half of what you've done, but—and this is important to remember—you will know it, and this makes writing your story so much easier.

Just remember, even if you do know it all, don't dump it all on your reader. If you must let them know it all, create an encyclopedia that you can self-publish or put on your website or make available some other way. This way, you can share it all without doing an info-dump on your reader.

I hope you had some fun with this. The nice thing about this is that you can use it again and again and create entire universes. Multiple universes.

The only limit is your imagination.

Congratulations on creating your world.

ABOUT THE AUTHOR

Vicky Burkholder has been married forever to the one person who accepts that she lives in a fantasy world most of the time. She's even been seen at the beach building worlds for her stories. In addition to creating fun characters, fantasy worlds, and suspenseful situations, she also enjoys and is very good at things like writing policy and procedures manuals and setting up continuity and organizational spreadsheets, both of which she has actually earned money doing. She has a master's degree in library science so likes things organized. Okay, so her family thinks having the spice rack alphabetized it a bit much, but she has no trouble finding what she needs when she needs it. And just because her extensive library is cataloged and organized, that doesn't mean she's obsessive. Honest.

When not writing, Vicky works as an editor, helping other authors with their works. When not doing either one of those, she can be found in the kitchen whipping up gluten-free, lactose-free, other allergy-free meals for her family. Or watching the world go by from her front porch swing.

You can find Vicky at: http://burkholv.wordpress.com

www.ingramcontent.com/pod-product-compliance
Lightning Source LLC
Chambersburg PA
CBHW071254280526
45788CB00004B/1721